First Ladies: The Life and Legacy of Hillary Clinton

By Charles River Editors

About Charles River Editors

Charles River Editors was founded by Harvard and MIT alumni to provide superior editing and original writing services, with the expertise to create digital content for publishers across a vast range of subject matter. In addition to providing original digital content for third party publishers, Charles River Editors republishes civilization's greatest literary works, bringing them to a new generation via ebooks.

Visit charlesrivereditors.com for more information.

Introduction

Hillary Clinton (1947-)

"I suppose I could have stayed home and baked cookies and had teas, but what I decided to do was to fulfill my profession which I entered before my husband was in public life." – Hillary Clinton

American presidents have shaped the course of global affairs for generations, but as the saying goes, behind every great man there's a great woman. While the First Ladies often remain overshadowed by their husbands, some have carved unique niches in their time and left their own lasting legacy. Dolley Madison helped establish the role of the First Lady in the early 1800s, Eleanor Roosevelt gave voice to policy issues in a way that made her a forerunner of First Ladies like Hillary Clinton, and Jackie Kennedy created glamorous trends that made her more popular than her husband. In Charles River Editors' First Ladies series, readers can get caught up to speed on the lives and legacies of America's most famous First Ladies in the time it takes to finish a commute, while learning interesting facts long forgotten or never known.

During the presidential campaign in 1992, Democratic challenger Bill Clinton announced that by voting for him, Americans would get two presidents "for the price of one." The reference to his wife Hillary signified that she would be no ordinary First Lady, and indeed she was employed frequently by her husband in the White House to try to push legislation through Congress, most notably universal healthcare. While that proved to be one of the Clinton Administration's greatest failures, Hillary and her staff continued to act as a political surrogate for the president during his two terms.

Of course, describing Hillary Clinton as just a First Lady belittles all of her accomplishments. Today she is the most powerful woman in the world and one of the most recognizable, working so seamlessly with her former rival Barack Obama that her popularity has easily eclipsed his within a year of his victory over her in the Democratic primaries. In addition to the stirring Democratic primaries of 2008, Hillary was a U.S. Senator from New York for nearly 8 years before becoming Obama's Secretary of State. Recognized as one of the sharpest minds in Washington and a complete policy wonk, Hillary has been one of the few bright spots in Obama's Cabinet during his first term.

First Ladies: The Life and Legacy of Hillary Clinton looks at the life and career of one of America's most influential First Ladies, but it also humanizes the woman who has overcome personal and political hurdles along the way. Along with pictures of important people, places, and events in her life, you will learn about Hillary Clinton like you never have before, in no time at all.

Hillary sworn in as Secretary of State, 2009

Chapter 1: Hillary's Early Years

On October 26, 1947, Hillary Rodham was born in Chicago to Hugh Ellsworth Rodham and his wife Dorothy Emma Howell Rodham, who were United Methodists. She is the oldest of three siblings growing up in a leafy suburb of Chicago, Illinois, a suburb named Park Ridge. Even from an early age, young Hillary demonstrated what kind of career she would have when she attended Maine East and Maine South High Schools, where she was known as a teacher's favorite, or, more pejoratively, "teacher's pet" as the expression goes.

The precocious teenager got involved in politics with gusto at a young age as well, but the woman who would become one of the faces of the Democratic Party was a staunch conservative in her early years. Growing up in a politically conservative household, Hillary canvassed neighborhoods after the 1960 election gathering evidence of electoral fraud in the extremely close Kennedy-Nixon race, and she was a "Goldwater Girl" in 1964, ardently supporting Republican presidential candidate Barry Goldwater. Hillary's father Hugh Rodham was an ardent Republican who detested the social welfare policies and the "Great Society" program of President Lyndon Baines Johnson, as he had detested President Franklin Delano Roosevelt's New Deal. But Hugh Rodham and his family were moderate Republicans who supported civil rights for African-Americans and were far from tried-and-true outright libertarians.

After high school, Hillary attended Wellesley College, the bastion of feminism, in Wellesley, Massachusetts. It may have seemed a curious choice for a conservative, but Hillary Rodham quickly found her eyes opened in a new and different direction from her Goldwater Girl days in suburban Illinois. Ever the daring person, Hillary went on a hike across the United States and was famously fired from a fish cannery in Alaska after complaining about the working conditions to the small business owner. The college girl was already displaying the social consciousness that has occasionally gotten Hillary into trouble, a strain of her character that led to the failure of her chaired health care commission in 1993, her allegation that "there is a vast right-way conspiracy" against her husband, and her efforts as United States Senator to seek protection for various groups, and so on.

The Era

The times undoubtedly were changing. This was the era of the Vietnam War, and the social stratifications — on racial, sexual, class levels — were simply breaking up or evolving to be more inclusive. This was also the peak of the Civil Rights Movement, and Hillary's future husband Bill Clinton was so moved and inspired by Rev. Dr. Martin Luther King Jr.'s "I have a Dream" speech that he famously memorized it. For her part, Hillary has been vocal about the fact that she left her father's and Barry Goldwater's Republican Party in order to champion the rights of the underprivileged, the environment, women, and children.

If it is true that the character of a person is shaped by the world as it is when they are twenty (as the Oscar Wilde saying goes), then the Vietnam War and Civil Rights Movement era are the lens through which Hillary Rodham Clinton sees the world. Significant legislative achievements during this period of the Civil Rights Movement — undoubtedly results of *Brown* — were passage of Civil Rights Act of 1964,[1] that banned discrimination based on "race, color, religion, or national origin" in employment practices and public accommodations; the Voting Rights Act of 1965,[2] that restored and secured voting rights for all Americans; the Immigration and Nationality Services Act of 1965,[3] that had less to do with then-citizens and more to do with potential future citizens and which substantially lessened the barrier to United States entry to non-European immigrants; and the Fair Housing Act of 1968,[4] which forbade discrimination in the sale or rental of accommodation.

Together these laws became known as President Lyndon Johnson's *Great Society Program*. Another component of this program was Johnson's nomination of Justice Thurgood Marshall, the NAACP's chief advocate in *Brown* and other cases, to the United States Supreme Court. Hillary would draw much inspiration from Marshall's life and his nomination. In 1993, at Marshall's funeral Hillary would sit with her Presidential husband on the front row of the Washington National Cathedral, poignantly staring ahead. Later that year (1993), when Bill Clinton would name his own first Supreme Court nominee (then-Judge Ruth Bader Ginsburg of the United States Court of Appeals for the District of Columbia Circuit) he would call her the "Thurgood Marshall of Women's Rights." Ginsburg's nomination was strongly supported by Hillary and she supposedly pushed her husband to nominate now-Justice Ginsburg. The connection with the *Great Society* era must have been significant in the minds of both Bill and Hillary Clinton and these perhaps were the terms according to which he wanted to frame his own presidency thirty years later. Hillary Rodham Clinton would be a substantial and probably indispensable part of that presidency.

Perhaps the most overlooked legislative provision -- as part of the 1964 Civil Rights Act – came after President John F. Kennedy's term (during President Lyndon B. Johnson's tenure) and upon President Kennedy's exhortation: 42 U.S.C. § 2000d (conditioning federal funds to non-discrimination in public services).[5] In requiring that programs that receive federal moneys end racial discrimination, by and large Congress has free rein.[6] There is evidence in the congressional

---

[1] 78 Stat. 252, as amended, 42 U.S.C. § 2000d *et seq.*

[2] 42 U.S.C. §§ 1973 *et seq.*

[3] Pub.L. 89-236; 79 Stat. 911.

[4] Pub.L. 90-284, 82 Stat. 73. C. Lamb & E. Wilk, *Civil Rights, Federalism, and the Administrative Process: Favorable Outcomes by Federal, State, and Local Agencies in Housing Discrimination Complaints*, Public Administration Review 418 (May/June 2010) ("the federal government's enforcement of national policy does not necessarily lead to the most favorable administrative outcomes for complainants — even in civil rights, where state and local governments have had poor records in the past.").

[5] "No person in the United States shall, on the ground of race, color, or national origin, be excluded from participation in, be denied the benefits of, or be subjected to discrimination under any program or activity receiving Federal financial assistance."

record that such evidence was being documented.[7] In greater numbers, African Americans re-entered politics in the South, and across the country young people were inspired to action. Both of these elements would elect Bill Clinton to the presidency in 1993, and he knew it. Nor would Clinton be allowed to forget this reality (and his wife Hillary would not let him forget it either). Through this Great Society era, the United States Supreme Court did uphold these federal laws as consistent with Congress's interstate commerce powers as well as its authority "to enforce by appropriate legislation" the Civil War Amendments.[8] Clinton as President would take the Supreme Court and his power to appoint likeminded judges very seriously, conducting much of the candidate research himself. It is doubtful whether that would have happened in today's climate, given the present Supreme Court's reluctance to readily embrace the congressional commerce power since the mid-1990's.[9]

Those issues are not dead and gone yet. Most notably, affirmative action — initiated by President Lyndon Johnson's Executive Order 11246 — continues to divide American society more as a fault line than a significant factor that makes a tangible difference. When Bill Clinton faced the choice in 1994-95 to support or overturn federal affirmative action, his wife Hillary and his African-American Secretary of Commerce Ronald Brown powerfully urged him to support affirmative action in the federal government's brief to the Supreme Court in *Adarand Constructors v. Pena* (1995). Many observers have commented that whereas middle-class and more socioeconomically potent African Americans and Hispanics are aided by affirmative action, poorer African Americans and Hispanics are not,[10] suggesting that society might be

---

[6] *South Dakota v. Dole*, 483 U.S. 203 (1987) (articulating that even though Congress's spending power authority is broad, it faces four limitations: (i) "the exercise of the spending power must be in pursuit of 'the general welfare'"; (ii) "if Congress desires to condition the States' receipt of federal funds, it 'must do so unambiguously . . . , enabl[ing] the States to exercise their choice knowingly, cognizant of the consequences of their participation'"; (iii) "conditions on federal grants might be illegitimate if they are unrelated 'to the federal interest in particular national projects or programs'"; and (iv) "other constitutional provisions may provide an independent bar to the conditional grant of federal funds.").

[7] 110 Cong. Rec. 1519 (1964) (statement of Congressman E. Celler, Chairman of the House Judiciary Committee) ("The bill would offer assurance that hospitals financed by Federal money would not deny adequate care to Negroes. It would prevent abuse of food distribution programs whereby Negroes have been known to be denied food surplus supplies when white persons were given such food. It would assure Negroes the benefits now accorded only white students in programs of high[er] education financed by Federal funds. It would, in short, assure the existing right to equal treatment in the enjoyment of Federal funds. It would not destroy any rights of private property or freedom of association."); *id.*, at 2467 ("In general, it seems rather anomalous that the Federal Government should aid and abet discrimination on the basis of race, color, or national origin by granting money and other kinds of financial aid. It seems rather shocking, moreover, that, while we have on the one hand the 14th Amendment, which is supposed to do away with discrimination, since it provides for equal protection of the laws, on the other hand, we have the Federal Government aiding and abetting those who persist in practicing racial discrimination.").

[8] *Katzenbach v. Morgan*, 384 U.S. 641 (1966); *South Carolina v. Katzenbach*, 383 U.S. 301 (1966); *Heart of Atlanta Motel, Inc. v. United States*, 379 U.S. 241 (1964); *Katzenbach v. McClung*, 379 U.S. 294 (1964).

[9] See, e.g., *United States v. Lopez*, 514 U.S. 549 (1995).

[10] S. Coate & C. Lowry, "Will Affirmative-Action Policies Eliminate Negative Stereotypes?," 83 AMER. ECON. REV. 1220, 1239 (1993) (stating that there is no clear indication that affirmative action actually works because "job preferences may induce employers to patronize the favored workers, which in turn may undercut their incentives to acquire necessary skills."); W. Bowen and D. Bok, THE SHAPE OF THE RIVER: LONG-TERM

suffering from a false sense of complacency about disparities. The real solution, they argue, is to institute better teaching methods in K-12 education and in the home, both of which are of course difficult without money. Affirmative action's supporters claim that it could not be unconstitutional because the 1866 Freedmen's Bureau Act, a federal law that gave many of its benefits just to newly freed slaves, was passed by the *same* Congress that had passed the Fourteenth Amendment,[11] thereby arguing that constitutional claims by disadvantaged whites are without merit.

Defenders of this racially-preferential interpretation of the 1866 Act pointed to the need for this sort of differential treatment and stated that for poor and socioeconomically disadvantaged whites "civil rights and immunities are already sufficiently protected by the possession of political power, the absence of which in the case provided for necessitates governmental protection."[12] In 1978,[13] throughout the 1980s and 1990s,[14] and quite importantly in 2003,[15] the Supreme Court had upheld race-based affirmative action only insofar as race was *one of many factors* and not a decisive or overwhelming factor. The Supreme Court has just recently granted review to decide the University of Texas undergraduate admissions affirmative action program in *Fisher v. University of Texas* (2011),[16] and given its current inclination the Court probably will use "equal protection of the laws" to repudiate affirmative action across the board.

CONSEQUENCES OF CONSIDERING RACE IN COLLEGE AND UNIVERSITY ADMISSIONS (Princeton Univ. Press, 1998) (arguing that an African American middle class has been positively affected and enhanced due to affirmative action in university admissions and silently leaving out any discussion of what has been happening to working class African Americans).

[11] 14 Stat. 174; see also Act of Mar. 3, 1865, ch. 90, 13 Stat. 507. Some Members of Congress were displeased that the bill was "solely and entirely for the freedmen, and to the exclusion of all other persons. . . ." Cong. Globe, 39th Cong., 1st Sess., 544 (1866) (remarks of Rep. Taylor). See also *id.* at 634-635 (remarks of Rep. Ritter); id. at App. 78, 80-81 (remarks of Rep. Chandler). Some Members opposed the bill on the ground that it "undertakes to make the negro in some respects . . . superior . . . , and gives them favors that the poor white boy in the North cannot get." *Id.* at 401 (remarks of Sen. McDougall). See also *id.* at 319 (remarks of Sen. Hendricks); *id.* at 362 (remarks of Sen. Saulsbury); *id.* at 397 (remarks of Sen. Willey); *id.* at 544 (remarks of Rep. Taylor).

[12] *Id.*, at 75 (remarks of Rep. Phelps). Had the Amendment (far more difficult to pass and ratify) than an Act of Congress been somehow *narrower in textual scope* than the 1866 Act, then there might have been a credible argument that Congress may have led by necessity to pass a narrower Amendment than statute in order to win greater support. Such an argument does not, of course, work here.

[13] *Regents of the University of California v. Bakke*, 438 U.S. 265 (1978).

[14] *Adarand Constructors, Inc. v. Peña*, 515 U. S. 200, 227 (1995); *Richmond v. J. A. Croson Co.*, 488 U. S. 469 (1989).

[15] *Grutter v. Bollinger*, 539 U.S. 306 (2003) (University of Michigan undergraduate and law school admissions).

[16] 631 F.3d 213 (5th Cir. 2011); *id.*, at 266 (Garza, J., specially concurring) ("Yesterday's racial discrimination was based on racial preference; today's racial preference results in racial discrimination. Changing the color of the group discriminated against simply inverts, but does address, the fundamental problem: [whether] the Constitution prohibits all forms of government-sponsored racial discrimination."); see also A. Keyssar, THE RIGHT TO VOTE 105–111 (2000); N. Persily, *The Promise and Pitfalls of the New Voting Rights Act*, 117 YALE L. J. 174, 208 (2007) ("The most one can say in defense of the [coverage] formula is that it is the best of the politically feasible alternatives or that changing the formula would . . . disrupt settled expectations"); *The Continuing Need for Section 5 Pre-Clearance: Hearing before the Senate Committee on the Judiciary*, 109th Cong., 2d Sess., 10 (2006) (statement of Richard H. Pildes) (stating that "the non-covered areas of the United States[,] . . . and, in fact, the evidence that is in the record suggests that there is more similarity than difference.").

What did the Vietnam War mean, especially for civil rights (the other change happening around now)? The War probably made Americans realize the necessity to give African Americans equal citizenship stature and also America's renewed need, just like during the *Brown* era against the Soviet Union, to show its in-house *equality* to guard against the North Vietnamese Communists's propaganda accentuating American *inequality*. Hillary appreciated these overarching trends as well as micro details. Bill Clinton also appreciated the importance of the changing attitudes to women's rights and roles (the Feminist Revolution) across the country and really the world, if not directly then through the wife (Hillary) he would soon meet. To Hillary, the civil rights movement always made eminent sense because of the 1960's climate in which it was situated. The racial and ethnic equality argument and the breaking down of stereotypes *on the racial basis* was not a new argument but it found a receptive audience by that time. To women like Hillary and Ruth Bader Ginsburg, the next step on the logical sequence of historical trajectory was women's liberation from domestic and inferior stereotypes — both in the public and private sectors. Bill Clinton, by listening intently to one and appointing another, would connect the two of them forever. These ladies would also find themselves listed among Most Influential Women rankings for decades.

Justice Ruth Bader Ginsburg

Hillary and Bill Meet, History Follows

After graduating from Wellesley, Hillary attended Yale Law School. Her final choice boiled down to Harvard and Yale Law Schools. When visiting Harvard, she was told by an arrogant professor, "We don't have any rivals and we don't need any more women." Hillary later acknowledged that was the moment that clinched the deal for Yale Law School in her mind, and it may have altered the course of history.

Naturally, Hillary was a busy body at Yale Law School, where she served on the editorial board of the Yale Review of Law and Social Action. In her second year, she also worked at the Yale Child Study Center, where she was a research assistant who helped produce the 1973 publication *Beyond the Best Interests of the Child*. The law student also volunteered at the Legal Services in New Haven to give free legal advice to the poor.

Hillary also got politically involved during her years at Yale. In the summer of 1970, she worked on Marian Wright Edelman's Washington Research Project, which provided her an assignment to Senator Walter Mondale's Subcommittee on Migratory Labor. In that role, Hillary learned about problems facing migrant workers, including housing, sanitation, health and education.[37] Edelman later became a significant mentor. Hillary even found time to work on the 1970 campaign of Connecticut U.S. Senate candidate Joseph Duffey.

During that same period at Yale Law School, Hillary was classmates with the future Justice Clarence Thomas, who would be appointed to the United States Supreme Court by President George H. W. Bush in 1991 to replace the epic civil rights icon and litigator in *Brown v. Board of Education* (1954),[17] Justice Thurgood Marshall. But it was a different classmate who would change her life and both reinforce and challenge her instincts: William Jefferson Blythe Clinton. Bill had been a Rhodes Scholar at Oxford who gave up his studies there to enter Yale Law School in 1970, a fortuitous choice for both him and Hillary. The next year, while sitting in the Yale Law School library, Hillary noticed Bill intently staring at her over the course of several days. Finally, Hillary came over to Bill and said that "If we are going to continue to stare at each other, we should at least know each other's names." Bill and Hillary would become *the* go-to power couple for decades.

---

[17] 347 U.S. 483 ("We conclude that, in the field of public education, the doctrine of 'separate but equal' has no place. Separate educational facilities are inherently unequal. Therefore, we hold that the plaintiffs and others similarly situated for whom the actions have been brought are, by reason of the segregation complained of, deprived of the equal protection of the laws guaranteed by the Fourteenth Amendment.").

Bill Clinton

Bill and Hillary have known each other for 40 years, and just what kind of a woman Hillary really is beneath the cool veneer is possibly one of the more secretive things that only her husband and daughter know. That makes their relationship, if not faithful (certainly not that), at least poignant and different. The relationship between Bill and Hillary might be one of the most dissected in American history, thanks to Bill's adultery, their seemingly insatiable ambitions, and the fact that they both seem to have alpha-dog personalities. In many ways, the Clintons are not just husband and wife or lovers or political partners; their relationship encompasses all of these roles and it seems to be something more. At this stage of their lives and careers especially, they seem to be friends who reinforce each other.

After graduating from law school, the Clintons moved in together; another unconventional step that 1960's *debutantes* just did not do before tying the knot in wedlock. According to Hillary, she took both the Arkansas and the District of Columbia bar exams. Having failed the District of Columbia bar exam but passed the Arkansas exam, she took it as a divine signal and moved to Arkansas to help Bill run for Congress. During this time Hillary was also acting as junior counsel to the Democrats in the United States House of Representatives in trying to investigate the Watergate break-in scandal implicating President Richard M. Nixon. President Nixon was forced to resign, and what no one (other than the Bill-Hillary inner sanctum) knew at the time was that Hillary's career was rising with Bill's. She was meeting not just prominent Democratic Members of Congress but she was also meeting people like Marian Wright Edelman, leader of the Children's Defense Fund (CDF), who would propel Hillary's career. In 1977, Hillary co-founded the Arkansas Advocates for Children and Families, a group in alliance with the CDF. President

Jimmy Carter appointed Hillary Rodham Clinton to the Legal Services Corporation (LSC), the group in charging of proposing as well as allocating funding to legal services for the economically under-resourced and underserved.

Chapter 2: First Lady of Arkansas

After leaving Yale with his law degree, Clinton spent just one year as a law professor at the University of Arkansas before trying his hand at politics. Running as a Democrat in 1974, Clinton lost his first race for the U.S. House of Representatives by 4% of the votes cast against incumbent Republican John Paul Hammerschmidt. What was extraordinary was his resilience. The very next day Clinton was in the town square's main street campaigning again.

Bill is often viewed as the greatest politician of his era, but his pre-White House steps did not come easy, and they almost did not happen at all because Hillary was seen as a bossy, officious, neurotic carpetbagger from the North with the candidate's ear, to the aggravation of Arkansans generally, including many Arkansas Democrats. In 1975, Bill and Hillary married, and for politically astute reasons Hillary took the "Clinton" name and became Hillary Rodham Clinton. Prior to this, she had always been known as Miss Hillary Rodham.

In 1976, Clinton ran for Attorney General of Arkansas and this time he won. Among other issues, Clinton began to support the death penalty fervently, a complete reversal of his earlier stance, and Hillary, despite her liberal background and instincts, understood political expediency when it was necessary. Bill would, throughout his political career, conduct on the death penalty issue what his legal hero John Marshall, the fourth and arguably the greatest chief justice of the United States, was accused of by Thomas Jefferson (Clinton's other favorite Founding hero): a "twistification."[18] Clinton appointed and supported the appointments of relatively progressive judges who would limit or strike down the death penalty while Clinton himself could be in agreement with the voters by strongly supporting the death penalty. This position would confuse his Democratic supporters in 1992 during Clinton's first presidential campaign, when Clinton would return to Arkansas to oversee the execution of Ricky Ray Rector, a death row inmate whose lawyers claimed was mentally retarded; the goal was to "code" and convey to independent voters that Clinton supported the death penalty, details of an individual case and its peculiar considerations notwithstanding. Many newspaper and press reports believed that Clinton wanted to eschew at all costs a "soft on crime" allegation that had cost him the 1980 gubernatorial election and went a long way to sinking Michael Dukakis in the 1988 election.[19]

---

[18] Letter from Thomas Jefferson to James Madison, 25 May, 1810, in Thomas Jefferson, *The Works of Thomas Jefferson*, ed. Paul Leicester Ford (G.P. Putnam's Sons, 1905), 11:141.

[19] A. Nguyen, "Bill Clinton's Death Penalty Waffle," *The American Prospect*, December 19, 2001, available at <http://prospect.org/article/bill-clintons-death-penalty-waffle> ("in 1988, Clinton . . . "told The Arkansas Democrat-Gazette, 'I can't say it's an inappropriate punishment for people who are multiple murderers and who are deliberately doing it and who are adjudged to be sane and know what they're doing when they're doing it.'").

Of course, the Attorney General's office was never the last stop for Bill Clinton, nor did Hillary want it to be. It was just the stepping stone. Both Bill and Hillary Clinton could tell that with President Jimmy Carter's unpopularity due to the oil crisis and liberal policies, it was time for a centrist "Third Way" and Clinton was branding himself and presenting himself to the public as a "New Democrat." In 1978, Bill Clinton won the Governor's office in Arkansas. He was only 32.

Governor Clinton and President Carter, 1978

As governor of Arkansas, Clinton worked extremely hard on educational reform in order to lift Arkansas out of its position as the lowest ranked state on education, and he also focused on revamping the state's infrastructure. He assigned Hillary to chair the committee on health care reform, a role in which she was largely successful by securing federal funds for impoverished areas. But Governor Clinton had also been forced to impose a rather disliked motor vehicle tax, and Arkansans also were upset with him over the fact that Cuban refugees detained in Fort Chaffee were able to escape state guards. In the 1980 gubernatorial election, Bill Clinton was defeated by Republican challenger Frank D. White, leading him to joke that he was "the youngest ex-governor in the nation."

In February of that same year, Hillary gave birth to daughter Chelsea, whose name was inspired by Joni Mitchell's song "Chelsea Morning" about the Chelsea section of London. The beaming ex-governor "bonded" with his new baby by walking her around the hospital and singing to her. Naturally, with two parents as busy as Bill and Hillary, young Chelsea spent a lot of her early years being baby sat by her grandparents, Bill's mother and the Rodhams.

In 1982, Bill ran again for the governorship in 1982, campaigning with an assist from both Hillary and Chelsea, who was included on car trips throughout the state. Clinton was elected governor once again in 1982, and this time he would remain in the state house for the next ten years. Though she was now First Lady of Arkansas, Hillary took up law practice as a partner in the Rose law firm, where she specialized in intellectual property law and patent infringement on her way to becoming the first woman to be made full partner in the firm. Hillary kept publishing law review articles ("Children's Policies: Abandonment and Neglect" (1977) and "Children's Rights: A Legal Perspective" (1979)) about children's rights, which have been criticized for their over-privileging of children's rights to sue their parents in court. The First Lady was making more money than the Governor.

As he had previously, Governor Clinton enlisted the help of Hillary. In addition to maintaining her positions as a lawyer and First Lady of Arkansas, Hillary also chaired the Arkansas Education Standards Committee, which successfully made a number of changes that completely reformed the state's education system, which rose from worst in the nation to one of the best. The Clintons accomplished this feat through several initiatives, including additional spending for schools, scholarship opportunities for gifted children (like Clinton himself once was), an increase in vocational education and teachers' salaries, and more stringent test requirements for those who would be teachers.

Bill Positions Himself on the National Stage

By transforming Arkansas' economy and raising the quality of public education in the state, Governor Clinton became a real leader among the Third Way New. The New Democrats, officially organized as the Democratic Leadership Council (DLC), were kind of a renegade or rogue branch of the Democratic Party that called for welfare reform and smaller government. Clinton also maintained a national profile as a prominent voice and leader among the Third Way New Democrats, which maintained a tricky balance with the Democratic National Committee and the more liberal wing of the Democratic Party, which included liberal stalwart and "Lion of the Senate", Ted Kennedy of Massachusetts, the Kennedy scion.

Despite the political differences within the Democratic Party, politicians like Clinton realized they would always have the support and votes of the far left simply because the Republicans would always be anathema. Moreover, as the New Democrats seemed to represent more mainstream positions, other members of the liberal establishment had to acknowledge, even if grudgingly, that Clinton and politicians of that ilk may be viewed in a better light. To that end, Clinton was asked to deliver the Democratic Party response to the immensely popular President Ronald Reagan's 1985 State of the Union Address and served as Chair of the National Governors

Association from 1986 to 1987.

All of this gave Clinton, who was still only in his late 30's, enormous exposure. Clinton positioned himself astutely by avoiding ideological battles of prior liberal eras and instead making his priorities economic expansion, job creation and educational reforms. To help senior citizens and thus invoke the Great Society as well as Franklin Delano Roosevelt's New Deal, Clinton got rid of the sales tax attending medications and expanded the home property-tax exemption. Hillary supported some of these ideas and opposed others but she was able to see that the candidate positioning himself as an electable Democrat, for the White House to boot, needed to make his own decisions.

In the important and extremely delicate project of making Bill Clinton acceptable to the Democratic Party's elders, Hillary's contribution has been overlooked. Not only was she a remarkable fundraiser but she provided Bill Clinton an important political asset. Among the Clintons, it was well known Hillary was the true liberal, and the fact that she had the future President's ear meant liberals sought to curry favor with her. Hillary was repeatedly sent to engage and mollify liberal Democrats who were upset with Bill Clinton's seemingly over-eager centrism.

Chapter 3: The Path to the White House

Given the strides Clinton had made on the national scene in the mid-1980's, many believed he might run for President in 1988, an opportune election that would not have an incumbent president. It seems Clinton himself considered it, and it was widely speculated that he considered a presidential run as a way to set up Hillary to succeed him as Governor of Arkansas. Ultimately, Clinton demurred, possibly at the behest of Hillary herself, and instead he stayed on as Governor, as well as heading the moderate Democratic Leadership Council from 1990-1991.

Clinton decided to run for the office of the President of the United States in 1992, but his campaign was nearly over before it began. After finishing a distant third in the Iowa caucus behind Iowa Senator Tom Harkin and presumptive favorite Paul Tsongas, Clinton's campaign was nearly derailed before the New Hampshire primary by Gennifer Flowers. Flowers came out with the explosive allegation that she and Clinton had been lovers for a 12 year period, forcing Bill and Hillary into damage control on the nationally televised 60 Minutes. Clinton did not exactly deny knowing her asserted that he had only had one sexual encounter with Flowers in 1977 and no more. Hillary stated, "You know, I'm not sitting here like some little woman standing by my man, like Tammy Wynette. I'm sitting here because I love him, and I respect him, and I honor what he's been through and what we've been through together. And you know, if that's not enough for people, then heck, don't vote for him."

Hillary immediately realized that her remark about Tammy Wynette was insensitive and politically damaging, and she now found herself a target during the campaign. As Americans and the press began scouring Hillary's own ideology, she came under fierce attack from conservatives, which would become a constant in her life for two decades. At the same time, Daniel Wattenberg's August 1992 article in The American Spectator compared her to Lady Macbeth, leading to a slew of similar articles drawing comparisons between the two.

Initially, the Flowers scandal seemed to push Clinton further behind Tsongas, a former Massachusetts Senator, in New Hampshire, where a bad loss may have ended Clinton's quest for the nomination. Instead, much like Hillary would revive her own presidential campaign 16 years later, Clinton made a surprisingly strong showing in New Hampshire, only losing to Tsongas in single digits. In the arcane world of politics, this was widely viewed as a victory for Clinton, who dubbed himself "The Comeback Kid" in his post-election speech. Newsweek magazine demonstrated how the media treated New Hampshire by running a cartoon with the Democratic and Republican runner-ups, Clinton and Pat Buchanan, wearing second place medals and standing on top of a victory stand while Bush and Tsongas wore gold medals off on the side.

With Harkin and Tsongas having won their native state and neighbor state respectively, the Democratic primaries were wide open, and Clinton seized control by sweeping nearly all of the Super Tuesday primaries, which included a host of Southern states. On March 17, 1992, as Clinton himself had predicted,[20] Clinton won the Illinois primary, which left him the clear frontrunner and proved he wasn't just a regional candidate. Tsongas dropped out, leaving only California's Jerry Brown as a potential contender. But Brown took stances like advocating a flat tax that were conservative positions well outside of the Democratic Party's platform, and with wins in New York and California, Clinton was on his way to securing the Democratic Party nomination.

---

[20]   Frontline: Interview   with   George   Stephanopoulos,   PBS   (2000),   *available   at* <www.pbs.org/wgbh/pages/frontline/shows/clinton/interviews/stephanopoulos.html> ("Oh, the smarts. The guy had thought everything through, both on the politics and the policy. When I interviewed for the job, it wasn't really an interview. It was me listening basically for an hour and a half to Governor Clinton just go through the entire landscape of the campaign. And in the very first time I talked to him . . . he said, 'It's all going to come down to Illinois on March 17. If I win the game in Illinois, I win Illinois, and I'll get the nomination.' That's exactly what happened. But he had it in his head back in September.").

As the Democratic nominee, it was time for Clinton's world-beating, dynamic campaigning skills[21] and sublime "inner confidence"[22] to take charge of the national election. President George H.W. Bush had seemed unbeatable at the height of the Persian Gulf War against Saddam Hussein's Iraq, with an approval rating near 90%, but a sluggish economy had pushed his approval ratings way down by 1992.

Throughout the summer, Clinton made serious inroads and took the lead over Bush for a variety of reasons. At the core, Clinton struck a stark contrast to Bush by appearing as a much fresher face and simply a smoother politician. While Clinton appeared on MTV and famously played the saxophone on the Arsenio Hall Show, Bush shot himself in the foot by expressing amazement at the way a supermarket could scan codes at the checkout aisle. The debates also put the contrast on display. Clinton connected with voters in town hall formats in a way few politicians ever could, while Bush was criticized for looking at his watch to check the time during a debate. And by putting the first President Bush on the spot by asking him the price of milk during a public debate (an answer that Bush did not at the time know), Clinton was able to make himself look like the "the People's Candidate" as opposed to the more elite and out-of-touch Bush.

---

[21] *Id.* ("We called him 'Secretariat' because he was just the absolute thoroughbred of thoroughbreds of campaigners. Whether it was working a rope line or giving a speech or devising the policy or just having the stamina to last through four 20-hour campaign days in a row and do it with good humor and grace. None of us had ever seen anything like this before. He is the politician probably not only of his generation, but if you're thinking just pure raw political skills, he's probably the politician of the century. And it was an awesome sight to watch.").

[22] *Id.* ("I thought it was just to be a terrific experience. That this was a smart guy who was going to move the party a little bit, bring ideas into the campaign and have a noble loss. Even if he got the nomination, George Bush looked unbeatable. But I thought it would be a terrific, important experience. But at some level, I think even if Clinton thought that maybe what he was doing was a sort of doing a practice run, he also had this unbelievable inner confidence.").

President Bush

Clinton polled at or above 50% for much of the summer until quirky billionaire independent Ross Perot entered the race and began polling around 20% himself, enough to give him a spot at the presidential debates. Perot and Bush took turns hammering Clinton on various character issues, including accusations of draft dodging, drug use, and womanizing. The Bush campaign also tried to present itself as stronger on foreign policy, with Bush famously telling a campaign audience, "My dog Millie knows more about foreign affairs than these two bozos."

But as Perot himself made clear with his famous TV programs full of charts, the economy was the main issue in the election. Clinton chose Democratic Senator Albert (Al) Gore, Jr., of Tennessee as his running mate and the two toured the United States promising a Third Way kind of "new beginning." While Hillary publicly supported the choice, it is difficult to know what she actually thought or whether she wanted someone more liberal. But by choosing another Southerner, Clinton ensured the ticket could not be attacked as out-of-touch "Northern liberals" like Dukakis, giving Democrats a chance to break the Republicans' grip on the South. Clinton never relinquished his lead in the polls throughout the Fall in the leadup to the general election.

Perot

Breaking a twelve-year long Republican stranglehold over the Oval Office, Clinton won the Presidency of the United States in November 1992 with 43.0% of the vote, as opposed to Bush's 37.4% of the vote and billionaire third-party candidate Ross Perot's 18.9%. The more significant number was 370 electoral votes, which was 100 more than what Clinton needed to win. Clinton's election represented a shift in the electoral vote of 517, compared to Bush's win in 1988, the second largest shift in history after Jimmy Carter's 1976 victory followed Nixon's landslide over McGovern in 1972. It was also the first time since Nixon's win in 1968 that a candidate won the presidency with less than 50% of the popular vote. Only Washington, D.C. and Arkansas gave the majority of their votes to a candidate (Clinton), while the other 49 states were won by pluralities thanks to Perot's candidacy. Bush's 37.4% was the worst an incumbent president had done in 80 years, when President Taft lost to Woodrow Wilson.

Chapter 4: A Tough Start

The First Lady reads to a child during a school visit

Scandals

From Chief Justice William H. Rehnquist, Bill Clinton took the oath of office on January 20, 1993 and got started on the job. In his inaugural address, Clinton reached for the inspiration brought on by boyhood hero John F. Kennedy's "Ask not what your country can do for you, Ask what you can do for your country" ethos and came up with "Our democracy must be not only the envy of the world but the engine of our own renewal. There is nothing wrong with America that cannot be cured by what is right with America."

Once the Clintons got settled in, both of them went to work on filling out appointments, and Hillary was part of Bill's innermost circle. She was instrumental in picking nearly a dozen top-level positions and dozens more for lower ones. It was clear from the beginning that Hillary was not going to be a typical First Lady, something Hillary acknowledged when stating that she sometimes had imaginary discussions with Eleanor Roosevelt. Early on, the Clintons were mockingly referred to as "Billary", indicative of the view that the two of them were co-presidents.

In the meantime, Clinton's still-young Administration was getting mauled by right-wing special interests as well as conservative members of Congress on scandal investigations. Much would be unearthed, but it would all be anti-climatic. Due to the Gennifer Flowers episode, Republicans smelled blood and wanted to see what else the searches and investigations might reveal about the Clintons. Whitewater was an easy target. Notably, in November 1993, a businessman named David Hale alleged that Clinton had behaved unlawfully years ago in the 1970's (while he was governor of Arkansas): Clinton supposedly had pressured Hale to give an unlawful $300,000 loan to Susan McDougal, a financial partner of the Clinton family, in the Whitewater land deal. The allegation against a sitting President (even for pre-Presidential conduct) was serious enough for a Securities and Exchange Commission investigation to occur. As a result of said investigation, Susan McDougal was convicted even though the Clintons themselves were never criminally charged. Both Hillary and Bill have always claimed they were entirely innocent of any criminal wrongdoing. Nor has any evidence shown that they were lying about this. In fact, when Kenneth Starr was appointed independent counsel in 1994, it was to investigate Whitewater.

Kenneth Starr

Other controversies came to the surface in the first few years of the Clinton presidency, including the 1993 suicide of Clinton family friend and Deputy White House Counsel Vince Foster. Despite wide-ranging conspiracy theories that Foster was murdered and/or that the Clintons covered up foul play, Starr's investigation corroborated the findings of an independent investigation that Foster had indeed committed suicide.

Months after Foster's suicide, "Troopergate" hit the headlines, with journalist David Brock reporting allegations by Arkansas state troopers Larry Patterson and Roger Perry that they arranged sexual liaisons for Clinton while he was governor of Arkansas, including with Paula Jones. Brock later recanted his piece in the American Spectator and personally apologized to Clinton, accusing the troopers of being "greedy" and having "slimy motives". Jones herself filed suit against Clinton in May 1994, alleging sexual harassment. Though the case would later be settled out of court, it was Clinton's testimony for the Jones case about Monica Lewinsky that eventually formed the basis for the charges used to impeach him in Congress.

Healthcare

In addition to these scandals, Clinton's early presidency and First Lady Hillary Clinton's reputation were both marred by the push for universal healthcare. A favorite topic of Hillary's back in their Arkansas days, President Clinton had tremendous confidence in his wife's ability to lead this project; after all, she had been billed by Clinton himself as "two for the price of one", and she had done a good enough job in Arkansas of delivering urban health care. But an extremely well-organized strategy by the insurance industry, political conservatives and even the American Medical Association (AMA) killed the legislative effort in Clinton's first year.

As shrewd as the Clintons generally are, they forgot four critical considerations: (*i*) State healthcare raises far fewer eyebrows than federal healthcare (larger territory, more diverse, much more contentious to establish, let alone manage); (*ii*) the Clintons were playing a greater stakes roulette and their enemies who hated them vehemently would stop at nothing to derail this item and thus to exact revenge or preclude work on *other* issues (many opponents had nothing to do with health care; they simply saw an Achilles heel they sensed was vulnerable); (*iii*) urban healthcare is not the same as general healthcare which people frequently see as intrusive and incursive of their personal liberty to make healthcare and HMO decisions; and finally, (*iv*) only the Clintons (particularly Bill) had found the whole "two for the price of one" tagline or even notion even remotely humorous or acceptable. Most people, out of sexism or a sense of the proper province of the Presidential spouse, thought the First Lady should stick to being White House hostess and a mute but smiling goodwill ambassador for the country. That was the traditional role that almost every First Lady, save for Edith Wilson (wife of President Woodrow Wilson) during the incapacitated days of President Wilson, had played up until that point. Voters too generally believed that their votes had been cast for *Bill*, not *Hillary*.

Over 15 years later, many political experts and pundits predicted the Obama Administration's push for healthcare was rather a losing effort like the Clinton Administration's had been. But Obama had never fully invested in the public option or the single-payer mechanism which seems to have been the Clinton Administration's almost non-negotiable starting point in 1993. When even a compromise legislative effort by the Senate majority leader Democrat George Mitchell of Maine failed in August 1993, it was clear that the reform was not going to pass then. And moreover Obama spent almost *all* of his political capital of his first few years in office on healthcare.[23] Clinton had not. Universal healthcare reform was the legislation that doomed the first few years of the Clinton Administration and caused significant losses of Democratic seats in both houses of Congress. Clinton would famously take the message from the midterm elections and announce in his 1996 State of the Union Address, "The era of big government is over". Though that is one of Clinton's most memorable soundbytes, the followup to that statement is often left out. Clinton continued, "[B]ut we cannot go back to the time when our citizens were left to fend for themselves. We must go forward as one America, one nation working together, to meet the challenges we face together. Self-reliance and teamwork are not opposing virtues -- we must have both."

Even still, Bill and Hillary were able to get some healthcare measures through Congress, even after the 1994 midterms. In 1997, Hillary and her staff pushed through compromise legislation that provided coverage to up to five million children through the State Children's Health Insurance Program (SCHIP). SCHIP wound up being the largest healthcare success of Clinton's presidency. Hillary also worked with Congress to pass the Adoption and Safe Families Act and the Foster Care Independence Act.

Other Legislation

Issues over which the First Lady's genuine views were unknown included trade protectionism, the death penalty, and gay rights, but even still Hillary lost much credibility with the Democratic Party establishment, whom she had wooed for Bill's sake, over his coming stances on these issues. The issues were important because they forced President Bill Clinton to take steps that his liberal supporters deemed stunningly retrogressive.

Although Hillary was furious at the healthcare setback, Bill was not deterred. Clinton fought hard for and was able to sign into law the Brady Bill (so named after the secret service protection of President Ronald Reagan who was paralyzed by a gunman's bullet intended to maim and/or

---

[23] There is a certain symmetry or coming full circle in the Clinton-Obama saga. It is also clear that the Obama Administration's domestic policy achievements in its first few years would have been close to nil had the United States Supreme Court nullified the Patient Protection and Affordable Care Act (PPACA), so insistently passed by the Obama Administration. Chief Justice John Roberts's controlling opinion in *National Federation of Independent Business v. Sebelius*, 2012 U.S. Lexis 4876, * (2012), upholding the crux (the individual mandate, requiring most persons in the United States to purchase health insurance or pay a penalty) of the PPACA. While Chief Justice Roberts rejected the more expected twin justifications, the Commerce Clause, U.S. Const. art. I, § 8, cl. 3, and the Necessary and Proper Clause, U.S. Const. art. I, § 8, cl. 18, thus jeopardizing a future course of Congressional action, he did form a majority with Justices Ginsburg, Breyer, Sotomayor and Kagan to uphold the mandate as an exercise of Congress's taxing power under the Constitution. Chief Justice Roberts, joined by Justices Breyer and Kagan, and with the combined votes of Justices Scalia, Kennedy, Thomas and Alito also struck down as exceeding the Spending Clause, Art. I, § 8, cl. 1, Congress seeking to withdraw, retroactively, state funds for States that refuse to accede to the Medicaid expansion authorized by the PPACA. See, *e.g.*, J. Rosen, "Welcome to the Roberts Court: How the Chief Justice Used Obamacare to Reveal His True Identity," *The New Republic*, June 29, 2012 ("Marshall achieved a similar act of judicial jujitsu in *Marbury v. Madison*, when he refused to confront president Jefferson over a question of executive privilege but laid the groundwork for expanding judicial power in the future.").

kill Reagan) on November 30, 1993. This statute imposed a five-day waiting period on handgun purchases throughout the United States. President Clinton also was able to expand the Earned Income Tax Credit, which essentially was a subsidy for low-income workers, and Clinton refused to flinch in the absence of Republican support for his tax bill, the Omnibus Budget Reconciliation Act of 1993 in August of that year, which passed both houses of Congress without a single Republican vote. In fact, several Democratic members of Congress are said to have been certain that with their votes they were signing away their electoral prospects in November 1994. The 1993 tax law reduced taxes for almost fifteen million low-income families, expanded tax cuts for 90% of all small businesses in the United States, and — much to the annoyance of the Chamber of Commerce — increased taxes on the wealthiest 1.2% of taxpayers. This is the same law that Clinton's immediate successor President George W. Bush would repeal and which the Obama Administration is now trying to reinstate. Additionally, through the implementation of spending restraints, it mandated the budget be balanced over a number of years.

Clinton also signed the North American Free Trade Agreement (NAFTA) (applicable to the United States, Canada and Mexico) into law, after the treaty passed Congress with narrow margins in both houses. This free trade measure also established extraordinary protections for investors of one signatory from the government of another. In what are called investment treaty arbitration tribunals, run by the International Centre for the Settlement of Investment Disputes (ICSID) and a few other organizations, investors may sue for high sums of money for the direct *or* indirect expropriation of some investment. This has included situations where market share or market access has been truncated by policies of the "host State." Protectionist Democrats, anti-trade Republicans and many supporters of the Green Movement opposed NAFTA because they viewed it as weakening the regulatory power of the State to protect human rights and to maintain environmental standards.

In 1994, President Clinton pushed for and saw to the finish line his Omnibus Crime Bill, which made countless alterations to existing federal statutes. The most significant of these changes was the sweeping expansion of capital punishments to include crimes not immediately causing death, such as running a large-scale drug enterprise. During Bill Clinton's re-election campaign he asserted, "My 1994 crime bill expanded the death penalty for drug kingpins, murderers of federal law enforcement officers, and nearly 60 additional categories of violent felons." As a former constitutional law professor at the University of Arkansas Law School, Clinton must have known that this statute conflicted directly with United States Supreme Court precedent — then and now.[24] He was, however, acting as a politician now. Never taking his eye off the political ball, Clinton's "twistification" served as a "code" to the public that he understood their problems while,

---

[24] *Kennedy v. Louisiana*, 554 U.S. 407 (2008) (there must be homicide or intended homicide in order for the death penalty to be imposed) (approvingly citing *Enmund v. Florida*, 458 U.S. 782 (1982), for the proposition that the Supreme Court "overturned the capital sentence of a defendant who aided and abetted a robbery during which a murder was committed but did not himself kill, attempt to kill, or intend that a killing would take place.").

simultaneously, appointing reliably progressive judges to the Supreme Court and lower federal courts who would invalidate such a law. His Supreme Court appointees, Justice Ruth Bader Ginsburg and Justice Stephen Breyer, have both been quite progressive (at least more progressive than not) on criminal law and gay rights issues. After all, his 1996 re-election was coming up, the same reason that he signed DOMA when the Republican Congress presented him with the bill.

Chapter 5: Hillary the Roving Ambassador

On the now ironic date of September 11, 1990, President George H.W. Bush addressed a joint session of Congress to explain why he was assembling a coalition of nations to intervene against Saddam Hussein's invasion of Kuwait. Bush stated, "Out of these troubled times, our fifth objective -- a new world order -- can emerge...A new era, freer from the threat of terror, stronger in the pursuit of justice and more secure in the quest for peace."

As his son would later attempt in another war against Iraq, Bush sought to present the coalition of nearly 40 nations as indicative of multilateralism, even though it was dominated by American forces. At the time, the Soviet Union was less than a year away from collapsing, leaving the United States as the sole superpower when Clinton came to office.

In fact, the "new world order" that Clinton stepped into was one that allowed for American unilateralism. Since World War II, the United States had protected the West during the Cold War, and Clinton's idol, President Kennedy, had coined the term "Pax Americana" to describe his hope of peace for the world. 30 years later, Clinton now had what he believed was the opportunity to use America's unchecked power to instill and preserve peace across the world.

However, Clinton soon learned this was much easier said than done. While his intervention in the Balkans was considered largely successful, he found trouble in Somalia, dead ends in the Middle East Peace Process, and terrorism from domestic radicals like Tim McVeigh and foreign enemies like Osama bin Laden.

Hillary is often viewed as a groundbreaking First Lady in the sense that she played an unusually active role in politics during her husband's two terms, but she was also particularly adept at traditional First Lady roles, especially in her travels. There can be no doubt one reason Hillary proved a popular and capable Secretary of State was that she was the one put out front and sent abroad to represent the United States, and she performed well and gracefully even in difficult circumstances. In March 1995, Hillary traveled without Bill on a five nation trip to South Asia, where she worked to improve relations with India and Pakistan.

In addition to promoting the Administration's interests, Hillary often addressed human rights during her travels. Her speech at the International Women's Conference in Beijing is remembered as one of her and the women's right movement's finest moments, where she declared "it is no longer acceptable to discuss women's rights as separate from human rights" and concluded "If there is one message that echoes forth from this conference, let it be that human rights are women's rights and women's rights are human rights, once and for all." She also gave voice to women's rights in Austria in 1997, stating, "We are here to advance the cause of women and to advance the cause of democracy and to make it absolutely clear that the two are inseparable. There cannot be true democracy unless women's voices are heard. There cannot be true democracy unless women are given the opportunity to take responsibility for their own lives."

During the Democratic primaries, Hillary would get in trouble for commenting that she and Chelsea arrived in Bosnia under fire and were forced to run for cover. Footage proved that was an incorrect recollection, and Hillary suffered a severe political black eye for it. Nevertheless, it is quite possible Hillary simply confused that with another visit, since she had taken countless trips as First Lady to places that ere indeed fraught with violence. A running joke in "Hillaryland" (the West Wing office Hillary used as First Lady) was that the President had a *de facto* policy: "If it is a dangerous place, send Hillary!"[25]

Chapter 6: The Lewinsky Scandal

In January 1998, a story broke that Clinton had engaged in sexual conduct with a 22 year old White House intern, Monica Lewinsky. Clinton flatly denied the story initially, notoriously remarking, "I did not have sexual relations with that woman, Miss Lewinsky." More importantly, he had made the same claim testifying in the Paula Jones suit. Hillary's reaction to the initial reports became famous as well. "From my perspective, this is part of the continuing political campaign against my husband... I mean, look at the very people who are involved in this. They have popped up in other settings. The great story here for anybody willing to find it, write about it and explain it is this vast right-wing conspiracy that has been conspiring against my husband since the day he announced for president."

Lewinsky, however, literally had proof of the affair, which she had discussed with friend Linda Tripp, and she gave the infamous "blue dress" to special prosecutor Kenneth Starr, whose investigation had now covered everything from Whitewater to Vince Foster to Paula Jones before seemingly stumbling upon a goldmine in Lewinsky.

That July, Clinton fessed up to the affair, admitting that he had an "inappropriate relationship" with the intern, though he continued to deny that it was a "sexual relationship", at least by his understanding of that definition. The political circus truly came to town, as Americans watched the former lawyer dance through grand jury testimony, including one famous answer in which he

---

[25] H. R. Clinton, LIVING HISTORY (2003).

discussed what the definition of the word "is" is. Clinton was never indicted for perjury, but he was subsequently disbarred by the state of Arkansas.

The Republican controlled Congress naturally thought Clinton had committed perjury and obstruction of justice, among other things, and began the process of impeaching the president. For only the second time in the nation's history (the first being Andrew Johnson during the Reconstruction period), the president was impeached by the U.S. House of Representatives in 1998, but eventually acquitted in the Senate after a twenty-one day trial in 1999. The nub of the charges — there were four charges in total[26] and only two (perjury and obstruction of justice) of

---

[26] H. RES. 611, U.S. House of Representatives, December 15, 1998, Article I ("On August 17, 1998, William Jefferson Clinton swore to tell the truth, the whole truth, and nothing but the truth before a Federal grand jury of the United States. Contrary to that oath, William Jefferson Clinton willfully provided perjurious, false and misleading testimony to the grand jury concerning one or more of the following: (1) the nature and details of his relationship with a subordinate Government employee; (2) prior perjurious, false and misleading testimony he gave in a Federal civil rights action brought against him; (3) prior false and misleading statements he allowed his attorney to make to a Federal judge in that civil rights action; and (4) his corrupt efforts to influence the testimony of witnesses and to impede the discovery of evidence in that civil rights action."); Article II ("(1) On December 23, 1997, William Jefferson Clinton, in sworn answers to written questions asked as part of a Federal civil rights action brought against him, willfully provided perjurious, false and misleading testimony in response to questions deemed relevant by a Federal judge concerning conduct and proposed conduct with subordinate employees. (2) On January 17, 1998, William Jefferson Clinton swore under oath to tell the truth, the whole truth, and nothing but the truth in a deposition given as part of a Federal civil rights action brought against him. Contrary to that oath, William Jefferson Clinton willfully provided perjurious, false and misleading testimony in response to questions deemed relevant by a Federal judge concerning the nature and details of his relationship with a subordinate Government employee, his knowledge of that employee's involvement and participation in the civil rights action brought against him, and his corrupt efforts to influence the testimony of that employee."); Article III ("(1) On or about December 17, 1997, William Jefferson Clinton corruptly encouraged a witness in a Federal civil rights action brought against him to execute a sworn affidavit in that proceeding that he knew to be perjurious, false and misleading. (2) On or about December 17, 1997, William Jefferson Clinton corruptly encouraged a witness in a Federal civil rights action brought against him to give perjurious, false and misleading testimony if and when called to testify personally in that proceeding. (3) On or about December 28, 1997, William Jefferson Clinton corruptly engaged in, encouraged, or supported a scheme to conceal evidence that had been subpoenaed in a Federal civil rights action brought against him. (4) Beginning on or about December 7, 1997, and continuing through and including January 14, 1998, William Jefferson Clinton intensified and succeeded in an effort to secure job assistance to a witness in a Federal civil rights action brought against him in order to corruptly prevent the truthful testimony of that witness in that proceeding at a time when the truthful testimony of that witness would have been harmful to him. (5) On January 17, 1998, at his deposition in a Federal civil rights action brought against him, William Jefferson Clinton corruptly allowed his attorney to make false and misleading statements to a Federal judge characterizing an affidavit, in order to prevent questioning deemed relevant by the judge. Such false and misleading statements were subsequently acknowledged by his attorney in a communication to that judge. (6) On or about January 18 and January 20-21, 1998, William Jefferson Clinton related a false and misleading account of events relevant to a Federal civil rights action brought against him to a potential witness in that proceeding, in order to corruptly influence the testimony of that witness. (7) On or about January 21, 23 and 26, 1998, William Jefferson Clinton made false and misleading statements to potential witnesses in a Federal grand jury proceeding in order to corruptly influence the testimony of those witnesses. The false and misleading statements made by William Jefferson Clinton were repeated by the witnesses to the grand jury, causing the grand jury to receive false and misleading information."); and Article IV ("Using the powers and influence of the office of President of the United States, William Jefferson Clinton, in violation of his constitutional oath faithfully to execute the office of President of the United States and, to the best of his ability, preserve, protect, and defend the Constitution of the United States, and in disregard of his constitutional duty to take care that the laws be faithfully executed, has engaged in conduct that resulted in

them received even a majority in the Senate, let alone a super-majority (two-thirds consent of the Senate being what the Constitution requires) — was that Clinton had lied about and had asked others to lie about his improper sexual relationship with Lewinsky.

Almost unbelievably, Clinton remained extremely popular among Americans, and his approval rating hit an all time high in the days after his impeachment. In the months after Clinton admitted to the "inappropriate relationship", the Democrats picked up seats in the midterm elections, a stunning rebuke that led to the resignation of Gingrich as Speaker of the House. On February 12, 1999, the Senate acquitted Clinton on both articles of impeachment, and Clinton had managed to outlast his political opponents yet again.

Clinton's presidency has been rated highly since the moment it ended, particularly for the peacetime expansion of the American economy during his two terms. As Americans are too painfully aware now, it was under President Clinton that the United States had a projected federal budget surplus for the first time since 1969. Not even the budget hawks during the Reagan and the first President Bush presidencies could claim this particular mantle, and it promises to be a very long time before a president hands over as solid an economy as Clinton left to incoming president George W. Bush.

When Clinton was replaced in January 2001 by President Bush, he left office with the highest approval rating for an outgoing president in 40 years. Now it was Hillary's turn.

Chapter 7: U.S. Senator Hillary Clinton

---

misuse and abuse of his high office, impaired the due and proper administration of justice and the conduct of lawful inquiries, and contravened the authority of the legislative branch and the truth seeking purpose of a coordinate investigative proceeding, in that, as President, William Jefferson Clinton refused and failed to respond to certain written requests for admission and willfully made perjurious, false and misleading sworn statements in response to certain written requests for admission propounded to him as part of the impeachment inquiry authorized by the House of Representatives of the Congress of the United States. William Jefferson Clinton, in refusing and failing to respond and in making perjurious, false and misleading statements, assumed to himself functions and judgments necessary to the exercise of the sole power of impeachment vested by the Constitution in the House of Representatives and exhibited contempt for the inquiry.") (relevant sections and excerpts of each).

Reenactment of Hillary Rodham Clinton being sworn in as a United States Senator.

Hillary's future role became clearer in 1998-99 when the legendary Democratic Senator from the State of New York, Daniel Patrick Moynihan privately told the White House that he would retire from the Senate in 2000 and not run for re-election. Giving ammunition to her critics that she was nothing if not an opportunist carpet-bagger, the Clintons bought a house in New York to satisfy residency requirements and Hillary decided to educate herself about New York issues almost as an intellectual project — one with enormous political rewards — and run for the office. Her political rewards were like Bill Clinton's running for and being elected Arkansas Attorney General in the mid-1970's; it was meant to be a stepping stone to greener pastures.

Hillary easily won the New York Democratic Primary and eventually defeated Republican Rick Lazio in the general election of 2000, becoming the first and only First Lady in American history to win an election and be a sitting United States Senator. That same night, as it would turn out, Vice President Gore, the Democratic nominee, would lose his bid for the White House against Texas Governor George W. Bush in one of the most contested presidential elections in American history. Famously the contest would go to the Supreme Court, resulting in the controversial *Bush v. Gore* decision.

As Senator, Hillary worked with some of the same people who had tormented her and her husband, but she immediately displayed her tactful skills and impressed everyone with her consummate grasp of the issues. After all, this was her big political test. Could she, not her husband, show herself in her own right to be a powerful, influential and dominant politician? Her issues were women's rights, children's rights, family policy and terrorism, brought about by the 9/11 attacks. Senator Clinton and her colleague Senator Charles E. Schumer made it their personal and professional crusade to gain money and support for the families of the 9/11 attacks, the fire-fighters affected by the recovery burnings and inhalation, and psychological help. In the wake of the attacks, echoing President Bush, Senator Clinton assured, "We will also stand united behind our President as he and his advisors plan the necessary actions to demonstrate America's resolve and commitment. Not only to seek out and exact punishment on the perpetrators, but to make very clear that not only those who harbor terrorists, but those who in any way aid or comfort them whatsoever will now face the wrath of our country. And I hope that that message has gotten through to everywhere it needs to be heard. You are either with America in our time of need or you are not."

Clinton had supported the 2001 invasion of Afghanistan, as had just about everyone, and she was in favor of the October 2002 Iraq War Resolution, which provided Bush authorization to use military force against Iraq if necessary to enforce a United Nations Security Council Resolution after pursuing with diplomatic efforts. That latter vote would definitely harm her during the Democratic primaries in 2008, but she explained her vote in 2003, stating, "I was one who supported giving President Bush the authority, if necessary, to use force against Saddam Hussein. I believe that that was the right vote. I have had many disputes and disagreements with the administration over how that authority has been used, but I stand by the vote to provide the authority because I think it was a necessary step in order to maximize the outcome that did occur in the Security Council with the unanimous vote to send in inspectors."

Of course, as things went south fast after the invasion of Iraq, Clinton and the Democrats found themselves no longer in lockstep with the Bush Administration. After the Iraq War began, Senator Clinton made trips to both Iraq and Afghanistan, visiting troops and learning about facts on the ground. Although Clinton was generally viewed as more centrist or hawkish than a lot of the other Congressional Democrats on foreign policy, she roundly condemned Bush's foreign policy by 2006, asserting, "The lost opportunities of the years since September 11 are the stuff of tragedy. Remember the people rallying in sympathy on the streets of Teheran, the famous headline — 'we are all Americans now.' Five years later much of the world wonders what America is now. As we face this landscape of failure and disorder, nothing is more urgent than for us to begin again to rebuild a bipartisan consensus to ensure our interests, increase our security and advance our values. It could well start with what our founders had in mind when they pledged "a decent respect for the opinions of mankind" in the Declaration of Independence. I think it's fair to say we are now all internationalists and we are all realists. This

Administration's choices were false choices. Internationalism versus unilateralism. Realism versus idealism. Is there really any argument that America must remain a preeminent leader for peace and freedom, and yet we must be more willing to work in concert with other nations and international institutions to reach common goals? The American character is both idealistic and realistic: why can't our government reflect both?"

Senator Clinton opposed the Iraq War troop surge of 2007 and voted in favor of a war-spending bill that required President Bush to begin withdrawing troops from Iraq by a set deadline, which Bush vetoed. Clinton opposed another measure that tied funding to an explicit list of benchmarks for the Iraqi government to fulfill, which was signed by Bush. Most famously, when General David Petraeus sent his September 2007 Report to Congress on Iraq, Clinton responded by saying, "I think that the reports that you provide to us really require a willing suspension of disbelief."

After being reelected in a landslide in 2004, it was clear that Hillary was positioning herself for a run at the White House in 2008, and she certainly had that in mind as she voted and voiced her concerns in the Senate. Hillary was handed another opportunity when the United States Supreme Court, by a 5-4 vote, rejected Lilly Ledbetter's equal pay and sex discrimination claim against Goodyear Tire and Rubber Co.[27] Hillary could now showcase her strong suit while positioning herself as *the* inevitable Democratic nominee for President.

Chapter 8: The 2008 Election

"From my perspective, you get up every day and you get out there and you make your case, and you reach as many people as possible. That's what I intend to do. So I'm in it for the long run." – Senator Hillary Clinton

On June 3, 2008, the final election returns came in for the Democratic Party's presidential primaries. With 18.2 million votes total, Hillary Clinton had won more votes than any other candidate in the history of the presidential primaries. The former First Lady was the first woman to make a serious run at the presidency, and she had been the overwhelming frontrunner to win the nomination at the beginning of the primaries.

That night, Barack Obama claimed victory, becoming the first African-American presidential candidate for either major party.

The race for the Democratic Party's presidential nomination was one of the most exhilarating elections in American history. John Edwards' campaign was rocked by rumors he had cheated on his cancer stricken wife. Bill Clinton, often referred to as the country's "first black president," was accused of racism in South Carolina. Video footage of Obama's reverend spouting anti-

---

[27] *Ledbetter v. Goodyear Tire & Rubber Co.*, 550 U.S. 618 (2007).

American, anti-Semitic sermons threatened to derail his campaign. And for half a year, a black man competed against a woman in a heavily contested race to see what kind of history would be made first.

Clinton narrowly won the popular vote, but Obama narrowly won the delegate count, making him the nominee.

How did all of that transpire?

With President George W. Bush suffering historic lows in his approval rating during the last half of his second term, political pundits widely anticipated that the eventual Democratic nominee would be the heavy favorite to win the general election in the fall of 2008. The Republican nominee would be saddled with an unpopular incumbent, and they would be campaigning just two years after Americans had thrown Republicans out of power in the House of Representatives during midterm elections.

On January 20, 2007, Hillary announced that she was forming a presidential exploratory committee for the United States presidential election of 2008, the initial step to run for the presidency. In the announcement she boldly asserted, "I'm in, and I'm in to win." Indeed, most people thought she would, and throughout most of 2007 she was well ahead of the other known Democratic challengers in opinion polls, including former North Carolina Senator John Edwards and current Illinois Senator Barack Obama. In September, Hillary was ahead in polls in the first six states to hold primaries, and the current primary logic is that sweeping the first two in Iowa and New Hampshire generally ensures the nomination.

However, by October Hillary was starting to lose her commanding lead, brought about in part by an uncharacteristically poor debate performance. Moreover, Clinton's aura of inevitability started to work against her, as Obama began working an angle of change to counter Clinton's assurance of experience.

In the important Iowa caucus, Hillary was dealt a stinging rebuke by finishing third behind Obama and Edwards in Iowa, and with that Obama was seen as a viable candidate. Obama gained considerable ground in national polls, and the polls indicated he would cruise to a comfortable victory in the New Hampshire primary. However, in a debate just days before, Obama made a crucial misstep by casually remarking "You're likeable enough, Hillary." And the day before the vote was held, Hillary nearly broke down while responding to a voter's question asking her how she did what she did. With tears in her eyes and her voice wavering, Hillary answered, "It's not easy, it's not easy. And I couldn't do it if I just didn't, you know, passionately believe it was the right thing to do. You know, I've had so many opportunities from this country, I just don't want to see us fall backwards - no. So - you know, this is very personal for me. It's not just political, it's not just public. I see what's happening, and we have to reverse it. And some people think elections are a game, they think it's like who's up or who's down. It's about our country, it's about our kids' futures, and it's really about all of us together. You know some of us put ourselves out there and do this against some pretty difficult odds. And we do it, each one of us, because we care about our country. But some of us are right and some of us are wrong, some of us are ready and some of us are not, some of us know what we will do to do on day one and some of haven't really thought that through enough. And so when we look at the array of problems we have and the potential for it getting - really spinning out of control, this is one of the most important elections America's ever faced. So as tired as I am - and I am - and as difficult as it is to try to kind of keep up with what I try to do on the road like occasionally exercise and try to eat right - it's tough when the easiest food is pizza - I just believe so strongly in who we are as a nation. So I'm going to do everything I can to make my case and, you know, then the voters get to decide."

All of this helped crack the façade that Clinton was an Iron Lady without emotions, and by showing herself to be human, she sprang a surprising upset victory in New Hampshire that ensured it would be a long primary.

With the primaries being close and hard fought, Clinton and Obama began to get more vicious with their attacks, which polarized the Democratic electorate. When Obama won a landslide in South Carolina on the strength of African-American votes, it was widely hailed as a victory made possible by racially charged comments made by Bill, Hillary, and other Clinton surrogates. Nevertheless, Hillary continued pressing on with her attacks on Obama, depicting him as naïve and inexperienced in debates and a famous commercial asking voters who they'd want to handle an emergency at 3:00 a.m. Hillary tried to push this difference between the two candidates, stating, "It's time that we move from good words to good works, from sound bites to sound solutions."

However, nothing Hillary could do broke the spell that Obama held over a significant bloc of Democratic voters, including minorities, young adults and college students. Obama nearly swept the primaries in February, also accruing delegates in barely contested caucus states to help bolster his delegate lead. Hillary held on in March by winning Ohio, and the following month she stayed afloat by winning Pennsylvania.

As Hillary fell further behind, she had to rely on the hopes that superdelegates would pick her despite Obama's lead in the delegate count. When it became clear that would not happen, Hillary officially conceded, despite having won more votes than Obama over the course of the campaign. In her concession speech, Hillary noted, "Although we weren't able to shatter that highest, hardest glass ceiling this time, thanks to you, it's got about 18 million cracks in it... You can be so proud that, from now on, it will be unremarkable for a woman to win primary state victories, unremarkable to have a woman in a close race to be our nominee, unremarkable to think that a woman can be the President of the United States. And that is truly remarkable."

With that, Hillary endorsed Obama and began to campaign on his behalf, helping bring her upset voters back into his tent after the bitter primary season by urging in her concession speech, "The way to continue our fight now to accomplish the goals for which we stand is to take our energy, our passion, our strength and do all we can to help elect Barack Obama."

After the Republican Party's national convention, McCain had a slight lead, but as the Great Recession began to reverberate with Bush still in office, the R next to McCain's name became too big a liability to overcome. Obama overtook McCain in the polls by September, and when Obama held his own in the presidential debates, enough Americans felt he was a safe choice.

At 10:00 p.m. on the night of November 4, 2008, the massive crowd in Grant Park exploded with joy. Barack Obama, a black man, had just been elected president. An hour later, the president-elect stepped onto a stage in the middle of Grant Park and told millions of Americans, "If there is anyone out there who still doubts that America is a place where all things are possible; who still wonders if the dream of our founders is alive in our time; who still questions the power of our democracy, tonight is your answer."

Chapter 9: Secretary of State Hillary Clinton

Hillary's first day at the State Department

Though Hillary had campaigned on behalf of Obama, their relationship was still widely assumed to be frosty, and it was an open secret that their campaign staffs openly hated the other candidate. Thus, it came as a shock to everyone when Obama persistently asked Hillary to be his Secretary of State. Hillary later related, "He said I want you to be my secretary of state. And I said, 'Oh, no, you don't.' I said, 'Oh, please, there's so many other people who could do this." Hillary was also worried that her famous spouse might be an issue that could compromise her work, noting, "There's one last thing that's a problem, which is my husband. You've seen what this is like; it will be a circus if I take this job"

Of course, Hillary's protestations aside, the selection made eminent sense. Hillary was a known policy wonk who would certainly master all the necessary portfolios, and it was the sort of role she had performed *unofficially* in her husband's Administration. By late November, Hillary finally relented and accepted, explaining how she reached the decision: "But, you know, we kept talking. I finally began thinking, look, if I had won and I had called him, I would have wanted him to say yes. And, you know, I'm pretty old-fashioned, and it's just who I am. So at the end of the day, when your president asks you to serve, you say yes, if you can."

Although many people anticipated Hillary might butt heads with Obama or make the State Department her own fiefdom, those concerns were put to rest almost immediately as Hillary went to work learning everything she had to and staying out of the headlines. She spoke with dozens of world leaders and shortly into her tenure claimed, "There is a great exhalation of breath going on around the world. We've got a lot of damage to repair." In her first 100 days, she had covered 70,000 miles across the globe.

Obama and Clinton at a NATO Summit

While promoting the Administration's interests, Hillary's celebrity status made her even more popular when she visited other nations, which also allowed her the opportunity to continue addressing human rights issues and voicing her opinions on matters outside her domain. "On their own, new technologies do not take sides in the struggle for freedom and progress, but the United States does. We stand for a single internet where all of humanity has equal access to knowledge and ideas. [...] The internet can help bridge divides between people of different faiths. As the President said in Cairo, freedom of religion is central to the ability of people to live together. And as we look for ways to expand dialogue, the internet holds out such tremendous promise. [...] We are also supporting the development of new tools that enable citizens to exercise their rights of free expression by circumventing politically motivated censorship. We are providing funds to groups around the world to make sure that those tools get to the people who need them in local languages, and with the training they need to access the internet safely. The United States has been assisting in these efforts for some time, with a focus on implementing these programs as efficiently and effectively as possible. Both the American people and nations that censor the internet should understand that our government is committed to helping promote internet freedom. We want to put these tools in the hands of people who will use them to advance democracy and human rights, to fight climate change and epidemics, to build global support for President Obama's goal of a world without nuclear weapons, to encourage sustainable economic development that lifts the people at the bottom up."

Within the Administration itself, Hillary formed a solid partnership with the first Secretary of Defense, Bob Gates, a Bush holdover that Obama kept in place. Together, they voiced more hawkish foreign policy views in debates about Afghanistan and Libya. Far from being at odds with Obama, Clinton has often been successful at persuading him to adopt her positions.

Hillary's success or at least prominence was most publicly underscored in the famous photo of the White House Situation Room where the President's team were watching the live footage of the Osama Bin Laden capture and killing. But the less well-known achievements of the Hillary Secretariat have been the trade agreements with various new nations, the *quasi*-freeing of the political dissident and democracy activist Aung Sang Suu Kyi in Myanmar (formerly Burma), and the advancement of women's rights conversations across Africa. The failures have been the continued impasse (and possible worsening of foreign relations) with Iran and North Korea, including the suspected enrichment of uranium for nuclear weapons.

Paradoxically, foreign policy successes and failures are often ascribed to the president, but Hillary has enjoyed her greatest popularity ratings during her tenure, with a far higher approval rating than Obama himself. In one memorable meme that Hillary herself enjoyed and endorsed, the "Texts From Hillary" spoof, photos of the Secretary of State showing her wearing shades and peering at her BlackBerry have been accompanied by captions in which the cool and assertive Hillary texts a bold statement to people like Obama, Mitt Romney or Arianna Huffington. Hillary herself turned it back on the meme's creators, sending in her own submission: More than anything, the "Texts From Hillary" meme weds the notion that Hillary is a dominant alpha dog with her seemingly newfound human side, as she seems to still be growing more comfortable in her skin even as she rises to new political heights. Indeed, it's impossible to imagine First Lady Hillary Clinton engaging in such humorous and unserious trivialities.

Hillary's own "Texts From Hillary" submission

As Obama has struggled with domestic concerns and certain foreign ones, some have openly speculated that Hillary would have been a better choice in 2008, and many held out hope that she would challenge him in 2012. For her part, Hillary has claimed she's no longer interested in running for president, but since she's resuscitated her image as Secretary of State, many anticipate and hope she will run for the presidency in 2016. Only time will tell, but it's clear that Hillary continues to be one of the most recognizable people in the world, and a force to be reckoned with.

Printed in Great Britain
by Amazon